C000240781

T 1

THROWING
A SICKIE

Dedicated to
Ray and Joy

First published 2004 by Boxtree
an imprint of Pan Macmillan Ltd
Pan Macmillan, 20 New Wharf Road, London N1 9RR
Basingstoke and Oxford
Associated companies throughout the world
www.panmacmillan.com

ISBN 0 7522 25014

Text © Tim Jones, 2004

All rights reserved. No part of this publication may be
reproduced, stored in or introduced into a retrieval system,
or transmitted, in any form, or by any means
(electronic, mechanical, photocopying, recording or otherwise)
without the prior written permission of the publisher.
Any person who does any unauthorized act in relation to
this publication may be liable to criminal prosecution
and civil claims for damages.

1 3 5 7 9 8 6 4 2

A CIP catalogue record for this book is available
from the British Library.

Design by Dan Newman, Perfect Bound

Printed by Bath Press

The Little Book of

THROWING A SICKIE

Tim Jones

BOXTREE

Introduction

52 weekends, 8 bank holidays, 20 days leave and 7 days sickday entitlement. That leaves 230 working days a year. The horror! To paraphrase Churchill, never has so much time been owed to so many by so few. We *need* sickies, and if you space them out and vary your excuses,

you shouldn't get fingered by
the boss. Just as well.

Reject guilt. There will be
times when you'll find it hard to
look in the mirror – and not
piss yourself laughing. But keep
focused, and the world is yours,
and all the afternoons in bed
you need. The Irish skive
St. Patrick's day – and he was
Welsh. The French and
Germans get 15 saints holidays.
If you're Italian, Greek or

Spanish, it's hardly worth going to work at all. So, be sick.

And *sound* it – the "I-am-sick-I-am-sick-I'll-sound-sick" mantra. Bosses will have little compunction about sacking malingerers – none if you're an accountant. So *believe* you have a malady – though not too much, or you'll get it psychosomatically and end up at the doc's – the last place you want to be on a sickday.

If you're rumbled, just cough, then hang up. Unlike the Samaritans, Personnel *cannot* call back. Just remember Machiavelli – "fortune favours the brave". Obvious really, and he made a living out of stuff like that. It also favours those with kids and pets, so claim to have them. Whatever, use the 200+ excuses here wisely. And enjoy your sickie!

1-5 days off **Back pain** – can't get out of bed? Blame your back. 90% of us get it, and it may require . . .

1 day off **Physiotherapy** – for future recurrence value, say that once your back goes, it's dicey. As Confucius say: "ah fuk, me bak".

1-5 days off **Flu** – if I need to explain this, you need your head examined. And sinuses.

1-2 days off **Asthma** – have an out-of-the-blue episode, then recurrent attacks (buy an inhaler from a pharmacist). This leads to . . .

1 day off **A consultant** – check out your

nearest chest clinic and cough.

1–5 days off Mild shingles – a viral infection in your legs where nerve-endings swell like chicken pox. Nice.

1–2 days off Allergic reaction to shellfish – skive a Thursday, so the blotchy

skin you report will have abated by Monday. The cause? The mysterious blackfish – plausible *and* total bollocks.

1 day off **Cricket concussion** – a Monday sicky. You were playing on Sunday and the ball hit your head.

3-5 days off **Crypto-spiridium –**

diarrhoea can arise from many sources – mostly the arse – and this water-borne bacteria.

1 day off **Paronychia –** para-what? You're half-way there! It's Latin and that's all Personnel need to know. It's a skin lesion that will go after *complete rest*.

1 day off **Vandalised car tyres/ windscreen** – you've got to call the garage, insurance company and police.

1 day off **You've hit a cyclist** – the bonnet's knackered and you're going with the police.

1 day off **The key's broken** – in the ignition. You're waiting for a locksmith.

1 day off **Been in a crash** – you had a blowout and are going to a garage.

1 day off **Your canoe fell off the car** – through the screen of

another car. You're giving a statement.

1 day off **There's a storm and you can't fly** – add an extra day to your supposed holiday by being subject to El Nino, or some other such bollocks.

1 day off **The train's broken down** – you're inside a tunnel and

the driver says there's been a cave-in.

1 day off **Blocked in by snow** – you're at your friend's Welsh farmhouse and a snowplough has pushed 10 feet of snow across his lane. And clearing it will be back-breaking work. Ahem.

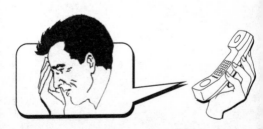

1 day off The ferry won't go – you're on the Western Isles of Scotland and the sea's too choppy. You'll be stuck for at least 15 hours.

1 day off The car drive-shaft has gone – you're now waiting for assistance. You could be

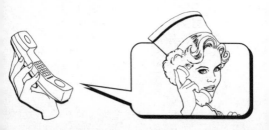

in any time. But not today.

1 day off **Allergic rhinitus –** headache caused by a constantly congested nose – requiring a visit to an . . .

1 day off **ENT specialist** who'll offer an operation; a Cottle's Device wire-steel coil; or

fucidinic acid cream. All
of them will fail and
require a second opinion,
who'll offer you all three
again.

1 day off **Wasp sting –**
you felt faint
and the surgery said to
take paracetomol and lie
down. All day.

1–2 days off **Nought
virus –** or

24-hour stomach bug.
Gotta go!

1 day off **Nose bleed –** leaving you light-headed and weak.

1 day off **Irritable bowel syndrome –** an undetectable condition that sprang from nowhere – other than the obvious. Case closed.

1 day off **Abscessed tooth** –
emergency treatment. It
will, of course, lead to . . .

1 day off **Nitrous oxide sickness** from
the gas. You feel groggy.

2 days off **Passenger in a car accident**
– you got minor whiplash
when you were hit by a
minicab – yeah, false

mahogony; tassles; Magic
Trees; Arabic mottoes.

1-2 days off **Sprained
ankle** – you
were playing football and
turned sharply. Buy a
cotton bandage and
linament for effect.

1 day off **Funeral
(extended
family)** – not all of them
(unless travelling refugee

class by cross-Channel lorry). Hoorah for uncle Bert!

5-8 days off **Funeral (nuclear family)** – all your relatives are alive – even the dead ones. Then, a sudden heart attack strikes. Again.

1 day off **Will reading –** your uncle Bertie's will.

1 day off **Your grand/parent has collapsed –** you're hospital-bound. Outcome? High blood pressure. Or sherry.

1 day off **Taking a relative for a**

hearing aid – what a waste of a day. Oh yes.

1 day off **Spreading ashes at a football ground** – uncle Bertie's, at Anfield. You can hear the Kop now: "He'll never walk again".

1 day off **Christening** – you should always be a god-parent – an alleged duty that'll

come in handy, I'll warrant.

1 day off **Collecting your niece from the airport** who's flown in from Australia. It's the least you can do, as her god-parent.

1 day off **Stag/hen do –** you went away for a weekend and, somehow, you've ended up

in Belgium. See you
tomorrow.

1 day off **Graduation –**
siblings, partner,
children. Claim they're all
doing a degree. Then a
Masters and PhD.

2-3 days off **Kidney
pain –** you're
having flushing therapy –
i.e. drinking cranberry
and pissing for Britain.

1 day off **Hernia** or
ruptured muscle.
Apply a menthol balm,
touch your stomach,
wince and go "oooh".

1 day off **Conjunctivitis**
– allergic
reaction to dust. Off to the
doc's. If you can find him.

1 day off **Blood in your
water** – you
don't want to talk about

it. Piss easy. A week later, say you ate too much beetroot.

1 day off **Cotton bud in the ear** – self-explanatory really. A&E.

1 day off **Blood test** – Personnel should be reticent about this. AIDS? Syphilis? Or something embarrassing? Like a paternity case.

1 day off **Piles** – another complaint afflicting 80% of us, Emma Freuds, Rockford Files, Nobby Stiles, Buddy Miles or, in medical parlance, "arse prunes" are a pain in the butt. Say your bum damsons are ripe and you've got to stick ice up your hole to shrink your veins into the

dark recesses. When this fails, hospital beckons for a . . .

1 day off **Vein splice –** a simple procedure involving the swift application of an ice-cold scalpel to your inner sanctum.

1 day off **Varicose veins –** the blood vessels in your feet

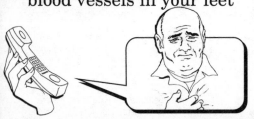

are protruding. Off to the doctor's.

1-5 days off **Pharyngitis** – another nice Latinism for the common cold. If they don't ask, don't tell 'em.

1 day off **Head in railings** – your son Terry's – through an iron fence. You'll be free when he is.

1 day off **Piano exam –** you're taking Terry, and it's 150 miles. Ridiculous, isn't it?

1 day off **Your friend's child is missing –** you're off to search for him. 4pm: thank God! He's turned up. Unlike you.

`1 day off` **Ingested bleach** – Terry's swallowed bleach. Yes, he *is* thick. And adopted. Hospital awaits.

`1 day off` **Head lice –** Terry has them, and you've got that itchy feeling you get when you just think about something itchy. Off to the chemist.

1 day off **Squirrel bite –** Terry. Yes, his nuts, etc. Hospital.

1 day off **Dog's muck –** Terry's swallowed some. Off to the doctor. "Why did he eat it"? He thought it was chocolate. "Is he blind"? No, but he could be.

1 day off **Its bark *wasn't* worse than . . .**
Terry's been bitten by a dog. Off to the doc for a tetanus jab for him, and a cyanide one for the dog.

1 day off **Diabetic reaction –** your child's had a diabetic reaction to chocolate. Ambulance.

`1 day off` **Child psychologist –** the beauty here is that *everybody* knows they talk bollocks, making this an on-going time-waster for years. Great!

`3-5 days off` **Tonsillitis –** penicillin. 'Nuff said.

2 days off **Allergic reaction to penicillin** – oh yes.

2 days off **Sciatica** – joint seizure. It'll pass, rest assured. As it were.

2-4 days off **Urinary infection** – from Polish vodka. Clinic and a small metal umbrella await.

1 day off You fell off a horse – onto your back. Ow.

5 days off Epizooti-glinfangitis – a horse disease passed from saliva. The symptoms – it makes you crap, sweat, ache, and jump over fences.

1-2 days off **Migraine –** the old aching nut. Could be genetics, age or cheese. So best avoid a non-organic mature cheddar. Lettuce has a palliative effect. But who wants to eat two icebergs when their head hurts? Anyway, you're incapacitated.

1 day off **A lump** – off to the doctor. Result? It was benign. Phew.

1 day off **Holiday jabs** – polio, diptheria, tetanus, typhoid, cholera, hepatitis C, malaria, yellow fever – a concoction that could lead to Gulf War Syndrome. Even if it doesn't, if you've been

pumped with enough
vaccines to keep a battery
hen going for a year, it's
no surprise you feel sick.

1 day off **Sub-navel rash**
— check-up. And
the result? That's private.
Or is it "bollocks"?
Actually, it's both.

1 day off **Birthday of
Guru Singh** –
which requires total rest.

Good job the moon wasn't waning or you'd be off a week praying to the Nepalese Walking Mushrooms.

1 day off **Mentoring** teenagers in residential care who have 'issues' – confidential ones.

1 day off **Territorial Army** – you've

been called-up, on an intelligence matter. Say no more.

`1 day off` Sponsored sick day – in solidarity with Great Ormond Street Hospital.

`1 day off` Rescue – Mountain/Cave Rescue or Lifeboat call-out on a Friday when

people go off for the
weekend. Like you.

1 day off **Tribal
chieftain** – you
were in Tanzania and
made honorary chief.
You've got to welcome the
tribe to this country.

1 day off **Hospital radio**
– you're on the
executive committee that
proposed increasing

membership fees. Some members reported you to the Charities Commission. You've got to explain yourselves to it.

1 day off **Neighbour-hood Watch –** you have to go to the police station for a briefing about being a co-ordinator.

1 day off **Your sponsored child** from Eritrea is flying into Britain and you've got to meet him at the airport.

1 day off **Religious conversion –** your friend Jack decided to convert to Islam. He got his foreskin chopped and *then* came to his

senses – seeing the apple on top of a beer bottle. He needs someone to vouch that he's switching back to Catholicism in good faith.

1 day off **Tinnitus –** ringing in the ears. Doc! Result? – just ringing in the ears. Transient. Not to say imaginary.

1 day off **Sleeping tablets** – that's why you're calling at 4pm. You had a migraine and took them by mistake.

5 days off **Diverticulitis** – or "shit fits". After a weekend to recuperate, you're fine. Strange that.

`2 days off` **Tetanus –** you cut your thumb with a fish hook. You got a tetanus jab and now feel ill.

`1 day off` **Vertigo –** you woke up and felt dizzy. You're not risking the stairs.

`1 day off` **Non-specific severe**

abdominal pain
(NSSAP) which affects
80% of us – a sharp,
burning pain that's
transient but requires an
examination. Note: health
scare + acronym = day off.

1-2 days off **Crohn's
Disease** – gut
pain that causes major
prodding by medical

professionals. Result? Probably NSSAP.

1 day off **You slipped –** on ice/oil, on your back.

1 day off **Mosquito bite** – a Monday call. You were bitten and it may be infected. Doctor! You don't want . . .

1 day off **Septicaemia –** blood poisoning. Like when you cut yourself on a rusty post. Penicillin awaits.

1 day off **Friend is suicidal –** their partner of eight years just walked out. You've *got* to go.

1-2 days off **Friend's funeral –**
heart attack. You're a bearer.

1 day off **Friend's wedding –**
you're best man/ bridesmaid.

1-5 days off **Neighbour's child is ill –**
single mum Mandy is rushed to hospital with

her gall bladder. You said
you'd look after Matthew
– who has nits.

1 day off **Friends spiked
your drink
with laxative** – gotta go.

1 day off **Your
neighbour says
they've got a poltergeist**
– you're off to get the
vicar.

1 day off **Neighbour's giving birth –** you've called an ambulance. No, she can't come to the phone.

1 day off **Friend's partner's gone berserk –** chucking clothes out. You're going over.

1 day off **You've been arrested** for sending a mate a joke parcel with "bomb" on it. They evacuated the sorting office, nicked your mate and asked for details of anyone who might have sent it. You're waiting for your solicitor – the other call.

1 day off **Your friend's been arrested** for putting spaghetti in his works' cisterns for a laugh. He needs you as a character witness.

1-2 days off Foot rot – from hill-walking marshy ground. You've got powder.

1 day off **Ceratitis** – an eye infection caused by dirty contacts. If you don't wear them, don't explain this.

5 days off **Acute Mountain Sickness** – following a supposed Nepalese holiday, get someone to call in re your AMS – which can kill. You're shitting

and vomming through
three orifices. End of story.

1 day off **Chlamydia** – a
downstairs
problem. Clinic.

3-5 days off **Ocular
histo-
plasmosis** – an eye
disease that makes you
feel fluey. Drops required.

1 day off **Chigoes –** following a supposed exotic holiday, your left arm is itching. Doc? It's chigoes – a flea under your skin. He's burned it out. Ouch.

1 day off **Kidney stones** – you had abdominal pain and called the doc. Result? Excess alcohol.

`3-5 days off` **Fifth disease** – or erythema infectiosum parovirus – runny nose, sore throat, joint pain, swelling. Should go soon. It will.

`1-3 days off` **Bacteriuria** – painful urination caused by a bacterium. Penicillin.

1 day off **Silent gallstones –** abdominal pain again. Check-up. And? Stomach cramps.

1 day off **Boiler's broken –** no heating or hot water. You're waiting for an engineer.

1 day off **Burglary** – call on a Monday. You were away at the weekend, and the lock's broken and your stuff's gone. You've called the police.

1 day off **Blocked drains** – the loo's backed up and you're waiting for the Council.

1 day off **Pipe burst –** waiting for a plumber.

1 day off **Mice –** there's a nest in a box of old toys. The bastards are in the Millennium Falcon and have chewed up some Jawas and Han Solo. You're laying traps, while clutching a light sabre.

1 day off **Hoover dust –** you were changing the bag and it burst. You feel nauseous.

1 day off **Oily feet –** you emptied the bin outside and walked oil over all your carpets. You're cleaning them.

1 day off **Electric cable severance –**

you were laying a speaker
cable and cut a main.
You're waiting for an
electrician and can't leave
'cos it's a fire hazard.

1 day off **New Zealand
flatworm** – a
botanist chum spotted a
worm on your acacia. He
made you call the
Department of
Environment as

it can devastate crops.
They're coming some
time. The result? No sign.
Must've been a trick of
the light.

1 day off **Wasps' nest** in
the roof. You're
waiting for Rentokil.

1-3 days off **Decom-
pression
sickness –** you went

diving at the weekend
and came up too quickly.

1 day off **Restless Leg
Syndrome –**
you've had pain and went
to the doc. RLS – muscle
twitches = tablets.

2–5 days off **Epigastric
mass –**
severe belly ache caused
by undigested food. You

need to rest. And open the windows.

2 days off **Mitral valve prolapse –** sounds serious. It's meant to. You had chest pain, and a check-up. Your atrial muscle's playing up. It's not a cause for concern; but is for two days off.

1-5 days off **Chronic Fatigue Syndrome** – you're on tablets. They should clear it, if you can be arsed to take them.

5 days off **West Nile Virus** – you had flu-like symptoms and then started wheezing. The doc says it's WNV (from your

parrot) which can cause fatal brain inflammation. You should be alright, though you might walk in a funny way if you hear the Bangles.

1-2 days off **Log-cutting** – you pulled your back out – it's saw!

1 day off **Log-cutting II** – a splinter in your eye. A&E.

1 day off **Air-bag** – you hit the brakes and the air-bag hit you. You feel dizzy. You're going to have to lie . . . down.

1 day off **Sick Building Syndrome** – you had bad flu. The doctor asked about work – central heating, air conditioning? He said it's

perfect for SBS and the company should improve conditions. Mention "class action", "out-of-court settlement" and "America", and your future sickies will be accepted far more readily.

1 day off **Parrot disciplinarian**
– Jarvis – he sounds like him – is swearing. A

psychologist is needed. Yes, it *is* necesary. Have you ever had *your* children called "wankers" by your pet?

1 day off **The dog's got roundworm –** off to the vet, who'll shove a heated wire up Luther's passage.

1 day off **Psittacosis –** you caught it

from Lionel, the macaw. A
form of flu.

1 day off **Daughter's horse trod on your foot** – it's sore.

1 day off **The horse threw you –** ooh, me back.

1 day off **Dog's given birth** in the

driver's seat of the car. You've got to clean it up.

1 day off **The dog's bitten sheep –** why? Ask Marvin. You're taking him to the police.

1 day off **The dog's died** – Percy. You've had him 12 years and are too upset (Oscar performance required).

1 day off **Dog's been hit by a motorbike** – Edwin. Vet awaits.

1 day off **Hyatid cyst** – you've had abdominal pain and it's a cyst, from dog saliva. The doc's prescribed medication, but if you start sniffing people's arses, pissing up lamp posts and shagging

people's legs, you'll have to call him back.

1 day off **Coughing up blood** – Doc. The result? A nose bleed you'd swallowed in the night.

2-5 days off **Donating bone marrow** for a cousin with leukaemia.

1 day off Radon gas – your neighbour's been ill for months and had his house tested. Radon. You're having yours checked. And? Clear. Oddly.

1 day off You shat yourself while driving in and now

you're back home. It's like you never left.

1 day off **Sunburn –** Monday. You were outside all Sunday and your back's burned.

1 day off **Water works –** causing you pain. Check-up. And? You're holding on too long.

1 day off **Open angle glaucoma –** you've had blurred vision, so went to the doc. He says it could be OAG – fluid on the eyeball – you've got to see an oculist. Result? Clear. Probably migraine.

1 day off **Mole removal –** not from the

garden – on your back, at
hospital.

1 day off **Sarcoidosis –**
you've been
wheezing and had chest
pain. Doc. And?
Sarcoidosis – mild lung
muscle disease. Nothing
you can do. Just grin and
bear it . . . and cough.

1 day off **Some kid spat**
in your eye –

you're worried about hepatitis B, so you're getting a jab. And that could make you ill.

1 day off **Nail in your foot** when laying carpet. Stupid. But effective.

1 day off **You breathed in fibreglass** when laying it in the

attic. Check-up. Result? Clear!

1 day off **Overcome by adhesive fumes** while laying roof felt.

1 day off **Sawdust in the lungs** inhaled while sawing shelves. Check-up. Result? Phlegm.

1-2 days off **Brown asbestos exposure** – you were in the attic and discovered it. Check-up. You know the rest.

1 day off **Paint fumes** have made you ill. They would.

1 day off **Broken finger** hammering a nail. X-ray. Result?

Bruising. (Wear a plaster in work.)

1 day off **Ants** in the lounge. You used a fumigator and breathed in fumes. Alternately, you've done an Ozzy and snorted them.

1 day off **Retaining wall** – the neighbours are renovating and have

knocked through. You're waiting for a builder.

1 day off **Fertiliser** – You were emptying a bag of lime and inhaled some. The usual.

1 day off **Numb hands/ shoulders –** you're going back to bed. Hopefully it'll just go. It will.

1-2 days off **Medical trial** – not the Shipman appeal. You're trying a new medicine and they give you £15 a day – and the shits.

1-2 days off **Chinese herbal remedy** – for hayfever, which has given you the squits. And visions of a dragon.

1 day off **Removal of ganglion** – an unsightly lump of tissue – on your left cheek (lower).

1 day off **Nervous eczema** in a sensitive area. You're off to the doc, then to lie down.

1 day off **Roundworm** – you've passed two feet of worm. Must be

from the dog. You're going to the doc's. Then vet's.

1 day off **Plasma cell dyscrasia** – you had a blood test re eczema and you've got plasma cell dyscrasia, which makes you feel faint occasionally. Funnily enough, this is one of those occasions.

`1 day off` **Dislocated thumb** – you did press-ups and slipped. Off to hospital, though there's nothing to see. Nor will there be.

`1 day off` **Chronic Obstructive Pulmonary Disease** – you've been breathless and coughing *Exorcist*-style. You're going to the

doc's. Result? An acronym. COPD – which means, a few days off. And tablets. If Personnel get too inquisitive, always bring up your phlegm.

`1 day off` **French cheese** – runs brought on by Cacquefort.

`1 day off` **Police ID participant** – you've been asked to

attend a parade re a robbery.

1-2 days off **Family history research** re a will. The archive's only open weekdays, and you've got to go in person.

1 day off **You've hit a farm animal** – got to get the car fixed,

report to the police, and
find a butcher.

1 day off **Crank calls**
from an Indian
man who says he wants to
"shag your bottom".
You're having engineers
in to change your number.

1 day off **Child porn on
your computer**
that you bought from a
car boot sale – stuff like

"Thumbelina, Thumbelina, tiny little quim". You're taking it to the police.

1 day off **Accident statement** – re a car crash you saw.

1 day off **Adoption hearing** – you want to adopt Terry but his parents object – in order to have a day out at

taxpayers' expense.
Result? They had their
day, we have Terry (and
his wonderful multiple
excuses for skiving work).

1 day off **Adjournment –**
re adoption.
Typical.

1 day off **Customs &
Excise
interview –** a mate's
been accused of dealing

hardcore porn. You're giving testimony that it's a mistake.

`1 day off` **National service** – you got call-up papers from the German Army. Apparently, one of your grand parents was half-German. *Now* gran tells us. You're going to the embassy to plead.

1 day off **Psoriasis –** suppuration on the thigh. 'Suppuration', if not up there with filovirus symptoms, is in the same league as 'phlegm'. Mind, if you say you've got Ebola and your eyes are bleeding and you're coughing up your lungs, they won't want you back. Ever.

`1 day off` **Ingrowing toenail –** pathetic, yes, but it's suppurating.

`1 day off` **Ringworm –** or strongybides stercoralis. The dog's had it and you've got an orange wart too. Doc, vet!

`1 day off` **Soft tissue sarcoma –**

saggy skin under your armpit. Check-up. And? It *is* a sarcoma but it's *not* malignant.

`1 day off` **Pain in the neck** – no, really – a mild thyroid condition causing transient pain.

`1 day off` **Weil's disease** – Monday. You went rafting on Sunday and swallowed river

water. You're worried
about Weil's from rats,
which can be fatal.
Hospital. Well? Yes,
thanks.

1 day off **Chorio-
retinitis –** Your
eyes hurt and it could be
a retinal disease. Oculist
beckons. You know the
result – migraine.

1-3 days off **Ulcer –** You've had abdominal pain. Doc. And? Helicobacter pylori. You're on tablets and have been told not to get stressed at work. Ho ho.

1 day off **Cytomegalo-virus –** your blood test re hayfever showed you have CMV –

non-sexually transmitted herpes. Clinic. Penicillin.

1 day off **Crabs** – clinic. No, you won't walk there sideways with your arms up in the air.

1 day off **Gas leak** – the gas company's told you to stay inside. Police will give the all-clear.

1 day off **A tramp's sleeping in the garden –** you're waiting for the police.

1 day off **Storm damage to a powerline** – winds have brought a tree down on a powerline and it's right outside the house. Waiting for the electricity company.

1 day off Water's contaminated and you've had the shits. You got a call telling you to boil water and apologising. But "sorry" for drinking other people's cack hardly covers it, does it?

1 day off Bitten by Terry's pal –

hospital – for a jab against lockjaw. Jab?

1 day off **Toxic plume –** the police say to stay indoors due to an accident at the chemical plant. Waiting for the green light.

1 day off **Crane hazard –** winds have swung its concrete-ballast

over your house. You're waiting for engineers.

1 day off **Unexploded bomb** – police said to stay in as road diggers have found what looks like a bomb. And? False alarm – an old gas cylinder.

1 day off **Suspected terrorist** – a man parked outside the

Army recruiting office, looking shifty. You spotted some bulky bags in the motor and recalled the old joke: why did the Irish chicken cross the road? BOOM! You've called the police. Result? The car was dumped after failing its test. And the bags? They were full of bags.

1 day off **Motor racing deafness** – on Monday. You went to the grand prix on Sunday and you're temporarily deaf. Eh?

1 day off **Haemo-chromotosis** – you felt faint and had a nose bleed. Doc! Result? Haemochromotosis – your blood-clotting cells are

low, due to being run
down by overwork. Iron
supplement.

1-2 days off **Scalding –**
the shower
scalded your left shoulder.
You can't dress. Ouch.

1 day off **Mushrooms –**
you picked some
while hill-walking and
made soup. You've been

throwing-up since. And
seeing pixies.

2-3 days off **Non-goniccal
urethritis** – you can't
pee. The doc's given you
tablets but it'll take a
couple of days' rest, *and*
exertion.

3-5 days off **A-strepto-coccus** –
sore head, throat, aching

bones. Doc! It's? A-streptococcus. Sounds nasty. *Sounds* it. Flu, to you and me.

1 day off **Gout –** you can't stand up due to lactic acid in your feet. Hopefully it'll just go. Though you never know when it might return.

1-2 days off **Mouth blister –**

suppurating. Doc. And?
From a chemical,
probably in a dodgy beer.
Ointment.

5 days off **Campylo-bacter** – you
had a Chinese meal and
have been sick. And the
doc says? Campylobacter
= the shits.

1 day off **Shin splints –**
lame, agreed.

But think of all those sick children you helped in that sponsored run.

5 days off **Seasonal Affective Disorder** – fluey, cotton wool head. Doc? SAD. There, there.

1 day off **Meteorite in the garden** – you've called the

observatory and are waiting – to flog it.

1-2 days off **Baby on your doorstep** with a note saying "baby". Waiting for the police.

1 day off **Invitation to meet the Queen** for your services to charity. Ahem.

`1 day off` **Bones** – you were metal detecting and found a buckle. Then bones. You called the police and have to show them the location.

`1 day off` **LSD trip** – you were on a stag/hen do, went to the loo, came back, had a drink, that's all you remember.

You woke up in Epping Forest. Or was it Uranus?

1 day off **Ransom note** for your mate Jack, in Colombia, from an insurgent group. You're taking it to the police.

1 day off **Treasure trove** – you were metal detecting and found coins.

You've got to fill in forms for the police.

1 day off **Pitbull** outside the door. It won't go. You're waiting for the police.

1 day off **Hypnotised** at a show on the weekend. You don't know why, but work isn't possible as you've got to shell peas for Somalia.

Now you've got to go and won't remember a thing about this when asked.

1-3 days off **MI5** have been following a drug gang and want to set up surveillance in your bedroom. Can't say any more – national security.

1-2 days off **Pregnancy/sympathy**

pain – you're pregnant, or your partner/sister is. You've got contractions, cramps, even (sympathy) Rockfords.

1 day off **Mesothelioma** – you've been getting chest pain. Doc. Diagnosis? Mesothelioma – a mild chest infection if treated early, which it will be. Before it starts.

1 day off **Waterbed sickness** – it could happen. You slept in a hotel and are motionsick.

3-5 days off **Leptopsirosis** – Monday. You went swimming on Sunday and have had vomiting, headache, chills, fever and aching muscles. GP,

please. And?
Leptopsirosis from
seaborne bacteria.
Tablets.

1 day off **Food allergy tests** at
hospital. Results? Allergic
to penicilin.

5 days off **Cyclic Vomiting
Syndrome** – sick during
the night. Call again later

and say the doc thinks it may be CVS – which can be short or long-term. Nice.

2-5 days off **Broncho-pulmonary aspergillosis** – you've been coughing, dizzy and losing weight. Doctor. Verdict? BA, caused by mould spores. Tablets await.

1 day off **Probiotic yoghurt** gave you Montezuma's revenge. "Feel right on the inside", my arse.

1 day off **Blinded by binoculars** when looking at a plane. You phoned the doc's and they say it should be transient.

1 day off Terry accidentally swallowed some Lego™. The doc says he should be alright longterm, but he could well be shitting bricks!

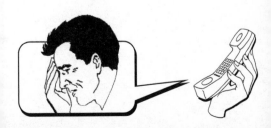

About the author

The author has never taken a sickie. He's also the man who single-handedly invented masturbation, led the 1980 'Icing Sugar For The People' riots, and won two VCs – at a tombola in Kensington. His previous work includes 'The Best Of The Ordnance Survey' (favourite grid-square, East Anglia south), carving the Easter Island statues when no-one was looking, and pioneering the 'Zhironovsky X' at the 1970 world noughts-and-crosses contest (causing a sensation not seen since the world Snap championship was halted by the German invasion of Poland).

He has gained a knighthood for services to empty churches, had a hit in Fiji with 'My Middle Name Is Gypsum Salts', and acclaim for inventing the "you're shit, ha" chant.

He currently lives in a world of his own.

A second volume will follow if he can take enough sickies to write it.